HOW DID WE GET OUR BIBLE?

AND IS IT THE WORD OF GOD?

Gary Bates
and
Lita Cosner

ABOUT THE AUTHORS:

GARY BATES is the CEO of *Creation Ministries International (US)*. He has been speaking on the creation/evolution issue since 1990, and has authored dozens of articles for CMI's popular website creation.com. His best-selling book *Alien Intrusion* is the only creationist book to have been a top-50 Amazon.com bestseller. He also authored the children's book *One Big Family* with his wife Frances; they have four children.

LITA COSNER earned an M.A. in New Testament from Trinity Evangelical Divinity School and works for *Creation Ministries International (US)* as its Information Officer and resident New Testament specialist. Her passion is explaining the Bible in a way that is understandable to the average Christian, as well as showing the unity of Scripture demonstrated by the New Testament authors' use of the Old Testament.

How did we get our Bible? And is it the Word of God?

Third printing: March 2018
© 2014 by Creation Ministries International (US)

Published by:

Creation Book Publishers
P.O. Box 350
Powder Springs, GA, 30127, USA.
Phone: 1-800-616-1264

creationbookpublishers.com

CONTENTS

WHAT IS THE BIBLE?
A Creator communicating with His creation

What if there was an 'instruction manual' for life that provided a foolproof blueprint for how we should live, that could tell us about realities outside of our visible universe and eternity, and provided answers to the big questions of life—would you be interested? Could it even be possible? After all, who would be qualified to write a book like that, and how could a book live up to such lofty claims?

Christians believe that the Bible was inspired by God, the Creator of the universe, and that He included all the information we need for life and how to have a relationship with Him. Because He created us and the whole universe, He is the only one who is really qualified to author such an essential 'handbook' answering life's big questions.

The Bible is actually a collection of 66 books authored by over 40 different individuals, who came from a diverse range of backgrounds. Some were fishermen, kings, prophets, warriors, scholars and even politicians. This is an important point. God desires a relationship with us, so He used and still uses, ordinary people to bring about His will and purposes. This is demonstrated in the Bible, where He chose a range of common folk like you and me to relate His words to us. Later in history, God Himself became one of us so we could understand His plan for humankind even more.

THE UNITY OF SCRIPTURE
And why it is important

The Bible is divided into the Old Testament (written from around 1400–400 BC) and the New Testament (c. AD 40–95). The word 'testament' used to simply mean 'contract' or 'covenant'—it's still used in the sense of 'Last Will and Testament'. The Old Testament records God's covenants with humanity before Christ, and the New Testament records God's covenant from the time of Christ onward. The first five books in the Old Testament are known as the Pentateuch (Genesis–Deuteronomy). These are often called by both Christians and Jews the written Law or Torah, but we shall see, they are also important historical books. Then come the 'historical books' (Joshua–Esther), the poetic books (Psalms–Song of Solomon), the major prophets (Isaiah–Daniel), and minor prophets (Hosea–Malachi). The Old Testament was originally written mostly in the Hebrew language, with a few sections in Aramaic. The two testaments are very much intertwined. The Old Testament looks forward to the coming of Christ and the redemption of humankind, and the New Testament records the fulfillment of all the hopes that the Old Testament authors wrote about, often referring back to them. The two testaments are really inseparable.

The New Testament is made up of the Gospels (Matthew, Mark, Luke, and John), which are four accounts of Jesus' life, His teaching or ministry, and His death and resurrection, written in the genre of *bios*, which is roughly analogous to the modern-day biography, but with some differences. The book of Acts provides some of the history of the early church. Then we have Paul's epistles or letters (Romans–Philemon), a collection of letters written by other apostles and early church leaders called the general epistles (Hebrews–Jude), and finally the book of Revelation, which is a record of a vision that John had about the end of this current universe, Jesus' return, and His ultimate defeat of Satan and sin. The New Testament was written in Greek, which was widely spoken in the Roman Empire in the first century.

The collection of all these books from the Old Testament and New Testament is called the Bible (from the Greek for 'book') or Scripture (from the Latin word for 'writing'). The Bible records an amazing amount of history, right from the creation of the world. Its authors were separated by different social standings (where they might not normally mix), sometimes by many hundreds of years, and sometimes by thousands of kilometers. Yet the whole Bible reads like one big continuous story and all of the books are very similar in their depictions of the nature of the Creator God, His love and His plan of salvation for fallen humanity. These unifying factors demonstrate remarkable evidence of the Bible's divine origin as God moved the authors to write under His inspiration. Also see the chart supplied (inside back cover) that demonstrates the amazing amount of cross referencing (over 2,800) that occurred between the books of the Bible. This highlights that the authors already believed many of these books to be of divine origin.

HISTORY
It's actually 'His story'

The Bible is an incredibly accurate history book. The number of ancient events, place names, and people groups it records that have been substantiated by other writings, historical records, and archaeological finds far surpasses any other book that claims to be an eyewitness account of history. Right at the beginning in the book of Genesis, it talks about the creation of the universe and the earth, and even events that will happen in the future (prophecy). The fact that it accurately prophesied future events makes it unlike any other history book written. But if God is the ultimate supreme author of Scripture, and the Genesis Creator, He exists outside of time and can therefore tell us about future events.

A lot of people grew up with 'storybook Bibles' as children, and so they've continued to view the Bible as a collection of 'fairy tales', even as adults. But the Bible claims to record actual events, and believing the Bible as real history is vitally important in understanding how we all came to be where we are today. Individually we all have a history. That is, there are events that occurred in our past, and we all must have a history of relatives or ancestors in our past. We know when we were born because there were eyewitnesses to those events, and most of us have a birth certificate signed by those witnesses. The book of Genesis is also really an eyewitness account of the origins of the universe.[1] It claims that the very first people, Adam and Eve, are the original ancestors of all people on the earth. Although it is beyond the scope of this book, modern science and the study of genetics is demonstrating this is very likely.[2] As scientific discoveries continue to show that all life is the result of mind-boggling, amazing, and complex information coded on the DNA of the cells of every living creature, the interconnectedness and biosphere of life on our planet has all the hallmarks of being purposefully designed.[3]

However, our world is winding down, and the Bible explains why the world is the way it is today. Genesis tells us that God originally created a perfect world with everything Adam and Eve (and us as their descendants) could possibly need. They only had to follow the rules God gave them for their own good, but they disobeyed because they thought they could judge what was good for them without God. This was the first sin. So if we want to define what sin is, we have to go back to the origin of the problem in the book of Genesis where we can see that humans decided to live their life as if God did not exist. This is still the major problem today and elements of this are present in every sin. And sin is not so much about the wrong things we do, but about the attitude that produces those wrong things—the wrong things are a symptom of the underlying problem—our sin nature. The ultimate problem is that sin offends God, who is pure and holy. It results in our separation from Him.

The entrance of sin into the world had devastating consequences. This event in history, known as the Fall of man, now means that bad things happen to us and our planet. People die; there are cancers, diseases, earthquakes and famines, and so on. Many people want to blame God for these things, but it is our fault (we can't just blame Adam, because we sin too, and human societies as a whole reject God). Humankind is reaping the consequences of rejecting a caring and loving Creator who made us in His image. We can't have it both ways. We can't reject Him and then say, "Why doesn't He do something?" The fact that we see bad things happening and that we all eventually die should be a reminder to us that something is terribly wrong with this Creation.

But even though our ancestors' actions caused the terrible curse of death that afflicts us, our loving God has indeed done something about our state, even when He didn't have to. Even before the Fall, God knew that it would happen, and planned a way for human beings to be saved from the curse of death and be reunited with their Creator. In Genesis 3:15 He pronounced to His adversary, a fallen angel named Satan who led, and continues to lead, humankind astray, that a deliverer (Saviour or Messiah) would come from

Eve's descendants. The majority of the Old Testament is a historical record of how God set aside a specific nation for Himself—the nation of Israel—that would eventually give rise to this Saviour—the Son of God, the Lord Jesus Christ. He gave this nation some very specific laws to live by, but no one could keep all these laws perfectly, thus proving again that we are helpless sinners in need of God's mercy. In other words, God's law was given to show people how sinful we are. Romans 3:23 says that "all have sinned and fall short of the glory of God."

The New Testament's history records the entrance of our Saviour, how we can be saved by believing in Him, and it also tells us that in the end this cursed world will be done away with, and a new heavens and earth will be created. Again, believing the Bible as real history is so important. For example, because of all of the promises (prophecies) of the Old Testament, we can recognize that Jesus is the Saviour that was foretold, because he fulfilled them (see some specific examples later). Also, if we believe that God is the Creator as described in Genesis, then it is easy to understand how Jesus could perform His miracles. After all, the Bible tells us that Jesus is God who came to earth, and therefore the very same Creator as described in the book of Genesis. The beginning of the Gospel of John says, "In the beginning was the Word, and the Word was with God, and the Word was God. … All things were made through him, and without him was not any thing made that was made" (John 1:1–3). Jesus is the Word of God, and the Bible is His Word.

It is important to understand that Jesus is the Creator, because only our Creator could save us. Also, it is important for understanding what He will do in the future, because if He made the universe once before, it will not be hard for Him to do it again when He restores everything. The culmination of this epic story is found in the Book of Revelation—the very last book in the Bible. It describes how God will redeem all those who believed in His Word and, thus, believed in Him. Believers are reunited with Him in a restored paradise where the curse of death does not apply, and so it will last for eternity.

A lot of people want to believe in God, but not what the Bible says about God, and particularly what it says about history, but there's no way to be consistent with that sort of 'pick-and-choose' approach. Jesus said, "If I have told you of earthly things and you do not believe, how will you believe when I tell you of heavenly things?" (John 3:12). The Bible's theology cannot be divorced from its history. If there was no real or literal good creation, and if Adam and Eve were not real people, and if their actions did not really bring sin and death into the world, then we really would not need to be saved from anything.

IS IT JUST A BOOK WRITTEN BY MEN?
The inspiration of Scripture

In 2 Timothy 3:16, the Bible claims that all Scripture is inspired by God or "God-breathed". If this is really the case, then of course this is what gives the Bible its authority. So, unlike purely human writings, the Bible claims to have a divine origin. Specifically, the Holy Spirit is credited with inspiring the prophets, both in the Old Testament (e.g. Nehemiah 9:20 says, "You gave your good Spirit to instruct them"; see also vs. 30; Isaiah 61:1; Ezekiel 11:5; Zechariah 7:12) and in the New Testament (Matthew 22:43; Acts 1:16; 6:10; 28:25; 1 Corinthians 2:13; 1 Timothy 4:1; Hebrews 10:15; 2 Peter 1:21; Revelation 2:7). Because the Holy Spirit inspired the very words of Scripture, it is accurately called the Word of God.

Some people think of the Holy Spirit as a sort of nebulous 'divine energy'—even referring to Him as 'it', but this is wrong, and misunderstands the Holy Spirit's active role as part of the Triune Godhead, and in the life of the believer. If you read especially the New Testament looking for mentions of the Holy Spirit, you will find that He is said to act in ways that only a personal Being could. The same Spirit who inspired Scripture indwells believers, and He has the role of interceding for us before God the Father (see Romans 8:26–27; Ephesians 2:18), teaching us (Luke 12:12; John 14:26; 1 Corinthians 2:13; Ephesians 3:5), and sanctifying us (setting us apart for God: Romans 15:16; 2 Thessalonians 2:13; 1 Peter 1:2). In other words, He helps us to be more like Christ and encourages us to live out what we're taught in Scripture. Isn't it a comforting thought that the Person who inspired Scripture lives in believers and will help us to understand what He meant?[4]

Contrastingly, the Bible says, "The natural person does not accept the things of the Spirit of God, for they are folly to him, and he is not able to understand them because they are spiritually discerned" (1 Corinthians 2:14). This gives us insight into why people reject or can't understand the Bible. If one truly wants to understand, he or she should pray for God's help. But if someone has already decided that he doesn't need God, is it any wonder he cannot accept His Word?

The Holy Spirit, like the other Persons of the Godhead, is outside of time. This is a difficult concept to understand because we exist in time (and space). But the very first verse of the Bible says, "In the beginning God created the heavens and the earth." This tells us that God existed before the universe that He made. Because we need a physical universe to define time (time is defined by change—the ticking of a clock, the rotation of the earth, etc, and this sort of change cannot exist without matter), He is not bound by what He created—He is eternal. He is also omniscient or all-knowing and therefore could inspire predictions of events that had not happened yet. An eternal being that is beyond the time of the physical universe can see the past, present and future. Even Jesus Christ, the second person of the Godhead is eternal. In Hebrews 13:8 it says, "Jesus Christ is the same yesterday and today and forever."

For example, consider passages such as Isaiah 40:22, which says about God, "It is he who sits above the circle of the earth, and its inhabitants are like grasshoppers." Some critics have claimed that the use of the word circle means that the Bible is incorrect because it is proclaiming the earth is flat. However, the Hebrew word is actually *khûg*, which correctly translated refers to the earth's sphericity or roundness. In any case, if an astronaut viewed the earth from space it would appear as a circle. Of course, the prophet Isaiah did not have the benefit of a spaceship to know whether the earth was a circle or a sphere. Only someone with a viewpoint from space (i.e. God) could proclaim such a thing. Similarly, in Job 26:7 he writes, "He [God] hangs the earth on nothing". These amazing pronouncements indicate a divine origin for Scripture.

In Luke 17:34–36, Jesus talks about his Second Coming. He says, "I tell you, in that night there will be two in one bed. One will be taken and the other left. There will be two women grinding together. One will be taken and the other left." This demonstrates that He knew about a round earth, by stating that different people on earth would experience night, morning and midday at the same time. How could any ordinary person know such a thing 2,000 years ago?

Further examples of the Holy Spirit's omniscience are demonstrated when He inspired the prophecy that the Hebrew nation of Judah would be exiled, but would be allowed to return after 70 years (Jeremiah 25:11–12; 29:10). And we see in Scripture that this was precisely fulfilled. He also inspired prophecy about Jesus. Sometimes this is directly predictive prophecy, but sometimes it is in the form of 'typology', meaning that certain people and institutions in the Old Testament foreshadow or resemble Christ in a certain way. For instance, God appointed priests to act as mediators between the Hebrew nation and Himself, and then later Jesus is called our high priest (Hebrews 4:14), and also our mediator: "For there is one God, and there is one mediator between God and men, the man Christ Jesus" (1 Timothy 2:5).

When we look at the places where the NT claims a certain prophecy was fulfilled, often they are talking about a typological fulfillment.[5] In the Old Testament alone, there are at least 46 specific prophecies about the Lord Jesus Christ that were fulfilled during His earthly ministry, death, and resurrection.[6] For example, in Isaiah 7:14 we read "Therefore the Lord himself will give you a sign. Behold, the virgin shall conceive and bear a son, and shall call his name Immanuel. (Immanuel means 'God with us')". Micah predicted that He would be born in the little town of Bethlehem (Micah 5:2).

GOD USES PEOPLE TO COMMUNICATE
The multi-faceted inspiration of Scripture

Even though there are these obviously divine aspects to Scripture, we can still see that it was a book authored by men. God often chooses mankind with whatever strengths and weakness we have, to bring about His purposes. When we look at Scripture in the original languages, we can differentiate between the styles of the different authors. In the NT, the Apostle John uses different words and sentence structure than Luke uses; Paul writes in the recognizable genre of the epistle for the purposes of teaching the early church. John wrote his Revelation in the apocalyptic genre as it relates mainly to future events. So, there are many elements, phrasings, and styles that wouldn't be explained solely by divine revelation, and that we would expect in a document written by human beings.

When God inspired Scripture, it was nearly always a combination of the Spirit and the human author creating the text, and we can see from a careful reading of Scripture that this works out in different ways. For instance, in some places, God seems to dictate to the prophet what he should say, like in Jeremiah 36. This was because Jeremiah was commanded to deliver explicit warnings to the people. But for the majority of Scripture, the human author seems to have considerably more control over the final product. However, it is important to state that this does not mean there are inconsistencies between authors when relaying the purposes of God or the big picture of the Gospel, in Scripture (see later about alleged Bible contradictions). For instance, Moses and Luke both seem to use pre-existing sources to write about events that they did not witness—this would require them to do their own research. Paul seems to be writing from his own mind, making intentional stylistic choices. For example, he writes "I do not want to appear to be frightening you with my letters. For they say, 'His letters are weighty and strong, but his bodily presence is weak, and his speech of no account'" (2 Corinthians 10:9–10).

And no one imagines the great King David taking dictation when he is writing the Psalms—he is writing out of the overflow of his own heart, in communion with the Holy Spirit, whether the psalm is rejoicing or mourning. So a biblical doctrine of inspiration has to take into account multiple levels of inspiration allowing for the text to also be shaped by the circumstances and culture of the authors. But no matter what level of independence the author seems to have, Peter confirms that the Holy Spirit 'carries along' the author of Scripture, making sure that he writes exactly what God intends (2 Peter 1:21), so we can be confident that God didn't allow any human error to contaminate the truth of Scripture as it was composed.

The big picture of the Bible details God's love and care for humans whom He created. It should not be surprising therefore that He should use humans to convey His message. God's method has always been to use people. The Lord Jesus became one of us so we could better understand who God is. Hebrews 1:3 says that Jesus is "the exact representation of God's being". Jesus also commands Christians to share their faith and take the message of God's love around the world, once again demonstrating that he chooses humans to convey his message to us.

HOW DO WE KNOW THAT THE BIBLE IS FLAWLESS?
The inerrancy of Scripture

Christians teach that the Bible, in its original manuscripts, is without error. This is important because the Bible is our source for knowing about God, His nature and our need for salvation. As such, it deals with the most important questions that every human will ever have to consider in his/her lifetime: Where did I come from? Why am I here? What happens to us when we die? Some people might ask if the Bible really is the words of a Creator God who can answer and do something about those three big questions. Therefore, if the Bible is in error regarding a comparatively minor point where we can check its claim, then how could we trust it when it refers to the future, or heavenly things where we can't examine or test these claims for ourselves (John 3:12)?

One of the most outstanding aspects of the Bible is its historical and predictive accuracy. History has shown many Bible prophesies to be true, such as Isaiah's prophecy that a Persian king would arise with the name of

Cyrus around 150 years before the event occurred (Isaiah 45). The Bible's historical claims have also been confirmed by numerous archaeological discoveries, such as the unearthing of a huge capital of the Hittites. These were an ancient people mentioned only in the Bible, but presumed to be a myth because no physical evidence had been found. As a result of these findings, the Bible has often been described as the most accurate history book in the world.[7] For example, a third generation female Israeli archaeologist called Dr Eilat Mazar stated "I work with the Bible in one hand and the tools of excavation in the other, and I try to consider everything."[8]

It is also important that the doctrine of inerrancy applies when the text is interpreted correctly according to the genre and context. When poetry is interpreted as poetry, and historical narrative is interpreted as historical narrative, and so on, the Bible will not convey any error. One also needs to be careful of simply reading things that attempt to discredit the Scriptures. It is very easy to pull things or even statements by the Lord Jesus out of context. We can't say, "The Bible clearly teaches, 'There is no God'", even though those exact words appear in Scripture 15 times. The reason, of course, is because in the context the text is saying, "There is no god beside me" (Deuteronomy 32:39); "The fool says in his heart, 'There is no God'" (Psalm 14:1); and "There is no God but one" (1 Corinthians 8:4).

Pulling passages out of context is something that people have tried to do for years. It is nothing new. But a truthful analysis will reveal that even though the Bible has been copied over many years, and via many translations, the big picture issues remain consistent and truthful to the nature of God and His purposes for mankind.

HOW CAN WE TRUST THE COPIES WE HAVE?
Transmitting God's words

Since inerrancy only applies to the original authored manuscripts, it is important for us to know that the copies we have are faithfully transmitting what was in the originals. We are not talking here about Bible versions, but the many thousands of copies in the original languages that date back many centuries.

From the time the earliest documents in Scripture were composed, they were copied so that more people could have access to them, and so that worn-out copies could be replaced. These copies had to be handwritten before the printing press was invented. In the case of the Old Testament writings, this task was performed by copyists known as scribes writing on animal skins sewn into scrolls.

THE MOST POPULAR BOOK EVER
The truth can change lives

The Bible is by far the most widely-read and the most published book of all time. In the last fifty years alone, it is estimated that over 3.9 billion copies of the Bible have been published. By comparison, the next most published book is *Quotations from the Works of Mao Tse-tung* (Mao Zedong) at around 800 million.[9] Chairman Mao, who died in 1976, was a Chinese communist dictator who ruled his country with an iron fist and imposed his socialist ideology on the populace. Given the current population of 1.3 billion and the imposition of his policies, the numbers are not all that spectacular. The next in line is not one book, but the series of seven books in the Harry Potter series at around 400 million.

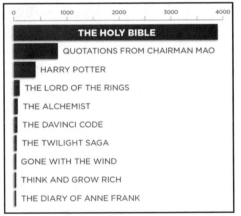

There are 5 times more copies of the Bible (4 billion) published than the next closest book.

Regardless of numbers, there is one statistic that really stands out. The Bible is also the most translated book in history. It is estimated that it has been completely translated into approximately 518 languages and that over 1,275 languages or dialects have at least some portion of the Bible.[10] We should not think of this as a solely human effort. In the same way that the Holy Spirit moved the authors to write Scripture, many men and women have been similarly moved to share the Good News of Jesus Christ to people groups all around the world. Countless missionaries have worked to translate the Bible even into the languages of small indigenous tribes that live in very remote locations. Individuals, families and even countries have been changed by the transforming power of the Gospel.

Even though the process of copying was time-consuming, there are more manuscripts of the New Testament than any other document. But in 1436, Johannes Gutenberg helped fashion the first printing press, changing the method of copying books forever. With moveable type and letters, this was a revolution for producing and distributing books. The first book ever produced on the printing press was, unsurprisingly, the Bible in c. 1454. It became known as the Gutenberg Bible and 49 partial or complete copies still exist today.

THE HISTORY OF THE WORLD
The Old Testament

For a long time, the oldest text of the complete Hebrew Old Testament that was available to scholars was from 1000 AD—this is called the Masoretic text, because scribes called Masoretes copied it. Critics claim that this text changed greatly from the original text, so much so in places that it was impossible to tell what the original looked like. (Today, we have copies of the Masoretic text that date from the 800s AD). However, even when the Masoretic text was the oldest Hebrew Old Testament available, there were good reasons to think it was a reliable copy—for instance, the Septuagint, which was a translation of the Hebrew Old Testament in Greek, was completed around third century BC, and much of it is substantially the same as the later Masoretic copies we have in Hebrew.

But in 1947, there was an amazing discovery made in Qumran, near the Dead Sea. Scrolls were found that formed part of a library of a Jewish sect that lived there. The scrolls included lots of non-biblical materials, but there were also books or parts of books of the Old Testament—in fact, at least part of every Old Testament book except Esther was found. These are known as the Dead Sea Scrolls and they date from the 200s BC to the middle of the first century AD. That means they are nearly 1000 years older than

Torah Scroll

the next-oldest Hebrew manuscripts we have. But there weren't lots of new Bibles published after the Dead Sea Scrolls were found, because generally, the biblical documents from Qumran match up really well with the Masoretic text, demonstrating that for over 1,000 years, scribes took great care with copying the text and didn't try to add to it or 'fix' it. So why would we expect this practice to have changed at all throughout all of history? Our modern translations of the OT are based on mostly the Masoretic text, but the Dead Sea Scrolls have helped to inform the newer translations in some places.

That the Old Testament text remained remarkably stable over time is not surprising. For one thing, professional scribes were the main copyists; they were trained to avoid the sorts of errors that are more common with amateur copyists. They also believed that they were handling the Word of God, and to eliminate the smallest 'jot or tittle' (Matthew 5:18; the jot and tittle were the smallest parts of the Hebrew letters) was to commit a grievous sin.

THE FULFILMENT OF GOD'S PROMISE TO MANKIND
The New Testament

The text-critical challenges to the New Testament are nearly completely the opposite from those of the Old Testament. We have lots of copies of the New Testament, and those copies are a lot closer to the time of the composition of the original document than the Old Testament copies. But more copies means more copying errors, especially since the New Testament was usually copied by amateurs.

The earliest copies of the New Testament date from the early second century—about 100 years after Christ. These are written on papyrus, a paper-like material made from weaving the flesh of plants, then pressing and drying it out. While it normally degrades quickly, under the right conditions like hot, dry climates that naturally aid preservation, papyrus can last thousands of years. We still have papyri that were made during the reign of the Pharaohs of Egypt over a thousand years before Christ. Even so, museums and libraries which house the papyri have to take special precautions to preserve these precious texts. The earliest fragments that we have serve an important function. Because they are so early, they are an indicator and confirmation for the accuracy of the parts of the New Testament they preserve, and by extension, the rest of the book.

The next-most important copies are the earliest complete copies of manuscripts. These date quite a bit later and they date from the 300s–400s AD. There are four 'Great Uncials' (named after a style of writing in uppercase letters without spacing between words), and they form the basis for much of the New Testament in the modern translations that have been produced since. There are other later manuscripts that are also important witnesses to the New Testament text, but generally the readings of the earlier manuscripts are preferred as more probably accurate.

Page from Papyrus 75

Manuscripts can be sorted into families based on the unique variants they have. The two major families are called Alexandrian and Byzantine, based on the geographic areas where they are found. The Alexandrian writings (named after the Nile Delta city in Egypt) are very early. Even though the manuscripts we have were preserved by the hot, dry climate in Egypt, there aren't a lot of them. The Byzantine text (named after the city Byzantium, then called Constantinople and now Istanbul) has a lot more copies to its name, so it's also called the 'Majority Text'. However, the earliest Byzantine manuscripts are from the seventh century, while manuscripts with distinctively Alexandrian readings go back to the fourth century AD. Both families, however, are very influential today and provide overwhelming evidence as to the originality and early widespread distribution of the NT.

Some Bible scholars specialize in looking at variants (different forms) of the text, and figuring out which is most probably the original. This is called text criticism (or 'lower criticism', not to be confused with historical criticism, or 'higher criticism'). People have been doing this for centuries—one of the most famous early critical manuscripts is the Textus Receptus created by Erasmus in 1516. He used the best manuscripts available in the 16th century. Today, our English King James Version, Authorized Version, and the New King James version are translations based on the Textus Receptus, and so was German reformer Martin Luther's German translation of the New Testament.

Codex Sinaiticus, one of the 'Great Uncials'

However, a lot has happened in the last 500 years in text criticism—we've discovered earlier manuscripts, and more complete manuscripts, which allows researchers to see a more complete picture of how Scripture was transmitted in the early church. For instance, Erasmus did not have access to a complete copy of Revelation in Greek, so he had to translate a Latin copy of the last part of Revelation back into Greek. Later we found manuscripts with the last part of Revelation, and unsurprisingly there are some differences between the biblical Greek and Erasmus' attempted recovery. For instance, Textus Receptus refers to the 'book of life' in Revelation 22:19, but all the Greek manuscripts of the last part of Revelation refer to the 'tree of life'.[11]

THE ANTIQUITY OF THE SCRIPTURES
Overwhelming evidence they have not changed

There are a lot of copies of the New Testament Scriptures—far more than for any other ancient work by a massive margin. Homer's famous *Iliad* (900 BC), for example, has about 643 existing copies with a 95% copying accuracy, yet there are over 5700 copies of the Greek New Testament. Next after *The Iliad* is Sophocles (496-406 BC) with 193 manuscripts.[12]

It is often claimed that there are so many differences between the different manuscripts that we can't really know what the New Testament originally said. But this is not really an accurate picture. These variants come from the 5700 copies of the New Testament, plus lectionaries, that were produced prior to the invention of the printing press—that's over 20,000 copies. When all that is taken into consideration, there are only an average of 20 distinct variants per manuscript.

It is important to remember that most of these variants are simply different spellings of words, and do not affect the meaning of the text. Other variants include changes in word order, or 'correcting' grammar. It is easy to see what the original wording would have been in most cases. The UBS Greek New Testament only includes 1200 variants as significant, and even in most of these cases, the original variant is clear, and the differences do not affect the English translation of the verse.

Only a few hundred variants are significant enough for Bibles to include them in the footnotes, involving less than 1% of the words in the New Testament; only a couple dozen involve a whole verse or two, and only two variants involve a larger section (Mark 16:9–20 and John 7:53–8:11). With all the massive efforts to ensure accurate transmission, we should be encouraged that God's Word continues to be accurately rendered to us. No variants affect Christian doctrine, because no belief rests on a single disputed passage.[13]

The rate at which the Gospels and the New Testament were copied and spread is simply stunning, and it's even more amazing that so many were preserved. It indeed indicates there was something special going on. It wasn't long before the church of Jesus Christ became the dominant influence in the culture of Europe and the Middle East. The same influence of Scripture has also underpinned all the great Western democracies. The message that God had saved mankind spread throughout the world. No wonder; it was Good News indeed!

WHICH BOOKS WERE INSPIRED?
And how did the church recognize them?

Both the Old Testament and the New Testament were composed alongside other documents that did not make it into Scripture. But it is important to point out that people don't determine whether or not a book is part of Scripture—the books of Scripture are those that God specifically inspired, and thus have the authority that divine inspiration gives them. So really, the question is not "how did the church decide which books to use?" but "how did the church distinguish inspired books from those that were useful but not inspired?" And as we shall see, from the beginning the early church was, in practice, already using these inspired books (they were also much closer to the date that many of them were written).

Both Testaments excluded later books that were deemed not to have been inspired. However, the Bible sometimes mentions these other books. For example, the Old Testament refers to the book of Jasher, the book of the wars of the Lord, and others which are not part of the canon. We should understand that any book can contain some truth, and the Bible deals a lot with history. Therefore we should not be surprised that it refers to other sources. The difference is that all of Scripture is truth.

There are also the 'Old Testament Apocrypha' books which include 1–4 Maccabees, Judith, Esdras, and others which did not make it into the canon. There are also books like the Shepherd of Hermas, the Didache, and the Odes of Solomon, which were written after the close of the New Testament canon—the time that the last book of Scripture (Revelation) was authored. Although some of these were widely used in the early church (because they may have contained parts that were helpful), they were never considered Scripture. So how did they distinguish the books that God inspired from those which, no matter how useful, did not have the same level of authority?

In the Old Testament, God spoke through prophets, and when they wrote something down, it was accepted as Scripture quickly, because it was recognized as God's word. One of the signs of a true prophet of God is that he should always be 100% correct if proclaiming God's Word. Using this as a benchmark, you can imagine that it was pretty easy to distinguish true from false prophets, as only God can truly tell the future.

Moses was the first author/prophet, and the five books he wrote, the Torah or Pentateuch (the Law of Moses), were the first canonical books. Of course the book of Genesis comprises narratives of historical events that occurred before Moses was born. Given the amazing propensity shown throughout history for preserving God's Word, it is likely that Moses had access to patriarchal records possibly preserved on clay tablets that were passed on generationally from father to son via the line of Adam-Seth-Noah-Shem-Abraham-Isaac-Jacob, etc.

And when a prophet's sayings were written down, usually by himself and then conveyed to the people, but sometimes using a scribe, that was also considered canonical. This formed a second group of writings known as the 'Prophets'. The third group is 'Writings', and that includes the Psalms, Song of Solomon, Esther, Proverbs, and other books that were not clearly prophetic in nature, but are nevertheless inspired. Some people say that this group was not 'solidified' until the hypothetical Jewish Council of Jamnia in the late first century, but first-century Roman-Jewish historian Josephus refers to the Scriptures being composed of 22 books before that. The divisions of the books were different, but the collection of the books coincide perfectly with our Old Testament, and this was decades before Jamnia, indicating that even if the canon had not been codified by the Jewish establishment as a whole, it was recognized by educated and informed Jews.

The New Testament books were written in a very short period of time—remembering that Christ was crucified around 30 AD, the earliest letters of Paul were written in the AD 40s, and the latest—John's Gospel and Revelation, were penned no later than the early AD 90s (and perhaps as early as before AD 70). This puts the entire canon within the lifetime of the apostles, and well within a century of Jesus' life, ministry, death and resurrection.

Some books were accepted as a part of the New Testament canon within the lifetime of the authors. The four Gospels that detailed Jesus' earthly ministry (Matthew, Mark, Luke and John) circulated early as a sort of 'mini-canon', and the completeness of their witness to the life of Christ was recognized, suggesting that this part of the canon closed early in Church history. The letters of the Apostle Paul formed another 'mini-canon', and there is evidence that they were also circulated as a set before the rest of the New Testament was collated. Other writings by apostles (Matthew, Peter's letters, John's writings) had automatic apostolic authority.

Though the canon actually closed with the writing of the last inspired book of the New Testament (Revelation) near the end of the first century, it took the church a little while to recognize which books were inspired (the full canon). There were a number of reasons, not the least of which was the overwhelming persecution that the church experienced during the first few centuries of its existence, which made circulation more difficult. Most of the books of the New Testament were recognized by around 170 AD when a document called the Muratorian canon was written. This document only exists in one fragment today, so we don't have the full thing, but its purpose was to affirm certain books and to clarify the nonbiblical status of others.

DISPUTED NEW TESTAMENT BOOKS
Are they valid?

Seven of the twenty-seven New Testament books were disputed in the early church—this means that there was some uncertainty in some places regarding whether they were actually part of the Bible. These books are as follows:

The Book of Hebrews: Unlike any of the other books, this book is truly anonymous; that is, there is no attested author either internally, or in the tradition about the book. The four Gospels are also anonymous, but there is no doubt who penned them, due to tradition (passed down) and the way the authors describe their relationships with Jesus.

With Hebrews, because the author is unknown, some were reluctant to ascribe biblical authority to it although it was in common use. In the East, it was considered to be Pauline, so was readily accepted, but it was not universally accepted until the fourth century in the West. This was due to the influence of Jerome and Augustine of Hippo (a bishop in the late 4th – early 5th centuries in the Roman province of Africa), and the belief that it was authored by Paul (despite the doubts of some Church Fathers). However, there is no doubt this book is inspired, and many consider it to be one of the finest epistles in the New Testament, particularly when it talks about Jesus Christ being the only mediator between God and humanity.

James: This letter claims to be from James, the brother of Jesus. He was not one of the original twelve disciples, but became a prominent leader in the early church in Jerusalem, as *The Acts of the Apostles* describes. Some disputed James' inclusion in the canon because it was claimed that it contradicted Paul's teaching about justification by faith. This conflict was still going on at the time of historian and Christian polemicist Eusebius in the third century AD. It was accepted as canonical in the West through the efforts of Origen, Eusebius, Jerome, and Augustine.

2 Peter: Because its style is so different from that of 1 Peter, some doubted whether they could have both been genuinely authored by the apostle. However, the use of a different amanuensis (a specific sort of scribe) to pen the letter, or simply the different occasion of the letter is plenty to explain the difference in style. Our sample of Peter's writing is much too small to say that something is not by Peter based on style alone, and since the book claims to be authored by Peter, we should take it at its word without any evidence to the contrary.

2–3 John: Both these small letters were addressed to private individuals and had only limited circulation. Because John identifies himself as an 'elder' in these letters and not an apostle, some doubted whether this was the same individual. But the second-century Muratorian canon nevertheless acknowledged its genuineness.

Jude: Written by another brother of Christ, this letter refers to the non-biblical *Book of Enoch* (14–15) and possibly also *Assumption of Moses* (9). Jerome, a theologian and historian in the 4th–5th century, specifically cites this as the reason why its inclusion was disputed. However, Paul's use of pagan poets is well-known and did not cause his books to be disputed, and Jude was widely accepted very early, starting in the mid-late second century.

Revelation: It is unique in that there is evidence that it was accepted in the second century, and only became disputed later. The third-century bishop Dionysius rejected it on the grounds that (1) the author did not make apostolic claims, (2) the arrangement and thought of the book is very different from the Gospel of John, and (3) the Greek of Revelation differs drastically from the Greek of the Gospel of John. However, there are good answers to all these points—for instance, because Revelation is apocalyptic, we would expect a different style of writing due to the staggering drama of John's visions. Also, the earliest tradition points to John the Apostle as the author of Revelation.[14]

THE APOCRYPHAL BOOKS
Why are they in the Catholic Bible?

If you've ever looked at a Catholic Bible, or even a really old *King James Version* (KJV), you'll notice that there are some extra books with names like 1–4 Maccabees, Esdras, and so on. These are called 'apocryphal' or 'deuterocanonical' books. They were included with the Septuagint, but unlike the rest of the books, they were originally composed in Greek, not translated from the Hebrew OT. They contain history, poetry, and wisdom literature from the time in between the composition of the Old Testament and the New Testament which was about 400 years.

For the first part of the church's history, no one considered these books to be part of the Bible—they're not in any of the earliest canons, and the Church Fathers don't quote them as Scripture. But when the Protestants split off from the Catholic Church during the Reformation, one of the big questions was: does the church have authority over Scripture (that is, does the church determine what is Scripture and how to interpret it?) or does Scripture have authority over the church? The Council of Trent was the first Catholic Council after the Reformation. It ran from 13 December 1545 to 4 December 1563, and in some ways it was a 'counter-Reformation' that corrected some of the abuses that were going on at the time in the Catholic Church, such as restricting public access to the Scriptures. But it also cemented some of the points of contention that caused the Reformers to leave the Catholic Church, and one of these things was adding the deuterocanonical books to the canon of existing Scripture. The Protestant Church grew out of the Reformation on the basis that the canon of Scripture, that is, the Word of God, was the final authority in all things.

Unlike some of the books composed in the post-New Testament era, the Old Testament apocrypha is not heretical, and even gives us useful information about Judaism between the times of the two testaments, which was about 400 years. But the apocrypha is not inerrant, it is not inspired, and therefore it is not Scripture.

TRANSLATIONS
Fulfilling the Great Commission

When Jesus gave the Great Commission, He told His disciples to "make disciples of all nations, baptizing them in the name of the Father and of the Son and of the Holy Spirit" (Matthew 28:19). This spurred on very early translations of the Bible into the languages of the various people to whom missionaries were sent. The original New Testament documents were written in Greek (itself the *lingua franca* of the day), but very early on it was translated into Latin, Syriac, Coptic, and other languages. Today, the New Testament is available in 1,240 languages, according to the United Bible Society.[15] This makes the New Testament by far the most-translated book in history.

There are two major translation philosophies. The first is called formal equivalence. Translators who hold this philosophy believe that a good translation should be 'word for word' as much as possible while still resulting in a grammatically correct product in the receptor language (the language into which Scripture is translated). The *New American Standard Bible* (NASB), *English Standard Version* (ESV), and the *King James Version* (KJV) are examples of 'formal equivalence' translations.

Another translation philosophy is 'dynamic equivalence'. Translators who follow this philosophy believe that meaning is encoded at the phrase level, not primarily at the word level. They believe that it is more important to get the original message of the text across, even if it results in using quite different words than a stricter translation would call for. The *New Living Translation* (NLT) is an example of a dynamic equivalence translation. Paraphrases of the Bible like *The Message* and the *Good News Bible* go further down the dynamic equivalence path, but they are so free with their wording that they are more accurately called "books based on the Bible", and aren't given the same status as translations.

While any particular translation can be said to be characterized by one or the other of the translation styles, no translation is 'purely' formal or dynamic equivalence. This is because there are elements of Greek and Hebrew that simply don't translate into English, or which sound very odd when stated 'literally' in English. This is sometimes because we don't have equivalent words in the English language. A 'word-for-word' translation of John 3:16, for example, would be "Thus for loved the God the world that the son the unique he gave, so that everyone who believes into him will not perish but have life eternal." We can see how the ESV's "For God so loved the world, that he gave his only Son, that whoever believes in him should not perish but have eternal life" is sufficiently 'literal', but at the same time puts the words into English grammar. The NLT goes a bit further, "For God loved the world so much that he gave his one and only Son, so that everyone who believes in him will not perish but have eternal life." The Message takes some liberty by saying: "This is how much God loved the world: He gave his Son, his one and only Son. And this is why: so that no one need be destroyed; by believing in him, anyone can have a whole and lasting life."

In the case of John 3:16, the more 'literal' ESV and other translations are preferable to the dynamic equivalence translations. But other times, an equivalent English expression brings out the meaning of the text more accurately than a literal translation. For instance, in Romans, Paul says in Greek, "*Me genoite!*" which translates literally, "May it never happen!" The expression is known as a 'divine passive', which means it's expressed in the passive tense, but meaning that God is the one who will keep it from happening. So when the KJV translates it "God forbid!" it is accurately conveying the message to the English audience more clearly than the NASB's "May it never be!", even though the NASB is more 'literal' at this particular point.

IS THERE A 'BEST' TRANSLATION?
Deciding what to use

Many people ask, "What is the best translation?" But that depends on a variety of things, which may affect what the most appropriate translation is. A translation like the KJV or the NASB may be above the heads of people who aren't used to reading at the level at which those translations are written. Some would suggest that the NLT might be better for someone who is coming to Christianity for the first time and hasn't learned 'Christianese' yet. But something like the ESV may be better for someone who really wants to get the best construction in English of what the underlying Greek and Hebrew are saying.

Really, the best translation is one that you will read, and can understand and apply to your life. Even reading from a few different translations, and perhaps a paraphrase now and then, can help you to see the multi-faceted meaning in some of the passages of Scripture. However, for serious study, a formal equivalence translation is preferable.

CORRUPT TRANSLATIONS
All Bibles are not the same!

Most translations of the Bible are sincere attempts to convey the meaning of the Greek and Hebrew originals. But there is one notable exception: the *New World Translation* (NWT).

The *New World Translation* was produced by the Jehovah's Witnesses, and they systematically edited Scripture to remove teachings that disagree with their teachers' interpretation of Christianity, and so they added things to the Bible, breaking one of the major tenets that brought the Reformation in the first place. One of the most infamous cases of this is in John 1:1. All the orthodox (doctrinally correct) versions of the Bible read, "The Word was God." But the NWT says, "the word was a god". This goes contrary to the Greek grammar of the passage, and specifically exists to deny the doctrine of the deity of Christ (and the doctrine of the Trinity). They translate the Greek word stauros, "cross," as "torture stake" because they do not believe that Jesus was crucified on a cross. There are far more other errors in this translation than can be listed in this brief booklet.

In addition, people continue to produce Bible 'versions' to fit certain predetermined ideological views. For instance, the *Queen James Version* was a 'translation' that corresponds with the KJV, except for key verses that condemn homosexuality; these were changed to remove that prohibition. On the other end of the ideological spectrum, the *Conservative Bible Translation* seeks to read a certain American political slant into the Bible, introducing inevitable anachronism and errors. No matter what the agenda is (or whether someone might personally agree with a particular view or agenda), it is always wrong for a viewpoint outside of the Bible to affect the translation of Scripture, because Scripture (our handbook) should be allowed to challenge and shape our thinking in all areas of life.

ARE THERE CONTRADICTIONS BETWEEN THE GOSPELS?
Dealing with the scoffers

In the ancient world, there was not so much interest about every aspect of a person's life, only the important, pivotal events. *Bioi* (the plural of the Greek *bios*) had to be accurate, but not necessarily chronological—stories about a person could be arranged topically (and this accounts for most of the chronological conundrums in the Gospels). Also, *bioi* did not tell an unbiased account of a person's life, the author had a purpose—you should revere Caesar as a god, regard this general as a war hero and a great man, or follow this philosopher's wise teachings. The goal of each of the Gospel authors is to present a different view of Jesus as God's Messiah—it was both to teach new Christians the core of Jesus' teachings and the history of his life, and to convert people.

Because the Gospels were written within about 50–60 years of Jesus' life, it's not long enough for a lot of mythical legends to have sprung up about Him. Eyewitnesses were still alive who could refute any false accounts.

There are some differences of wording in the Gospels in places. This is because the disciples memorized Jesus' teachings, and then translated them. Jesus taught in either Aramaic or Hebrew. By analogy, if four different people translated the Constitution of the United States into Spanish, we would expect there to be some differences, simply due to the nature of translation. But the essence of the teachings is the same. It's not like Mark teaches something contradictory to Matthew.

WERE THE GOSPELS ALTERED?
Or were the prophecies intentionally fulfilled?

Over the years many Bible skeptics have claimed that Jesus tried to purposely fulfill the Old Testament prophecies about the coming Messiah, or that the New Testament writers wrote the Gospels with the intent of making them apply to Jesus.

Earlier, we mentioned that there were at least 46 specific prophecies about Jesus that were fulfilled during His earthly ministry. Many lists have well over 100, so 46 is a conservative estimate. In a book called *Science Speaks,* Professor Peter Stoner and Dr Robert Newman calculated the chances of just eight prophecies being fulfilled by chance. For example, regarding the prophecy in Micah 5:2 that the Messiah would be born in the town of Bethlehem, they estimated what the chances were, based on the population of the world and Bethlehem at that time, someone might happen to be born there by chance. Or, in calculating Jesus' betrayal by Judas for thirty pieces of silver (Zechariah 11:12) they asked of all the people that have ever been betrayed, how many may have been betrayed for exactly thirty silver coins, and so on.

In calculating the estimates of just one man fulfilling just eight prophecies they estimated the chances to be 1 in 10^{28}. That's a staggering 1 in 10,000,000,000,000,000,000,000,000,000. Or to put it another way, it would be the same chance as a blindfolded person picking the right silver dollar at random—out of 10^{17} (that's enough to cover the state of Texas two feet deep in silver dollars).

Probability arguments can be somewhat arbitrary due to the selection of criteria and the assumptions made for starting conditions. However, with the above arguments, the manuscript for *Science Speaks* was carefully reviewed by a committee of the American Scientific Affiliation, who endorsed the accuracy of their argument.[16]

And remember we were only talking about 8 prophecies, not our estimate of 46! So it is not realistic to argue that Jesus just happened to be in the right place at the right time so often, or in reality, 'the wrong place so often' given the horrible method of crucifixion that He underwent.

So what about the idea that the Gospel writers made up stories to fit the prophecies? We've already pointed out the painstaking propensity of the Jews for preserving historical records, precisely because they believed them to be true events. To believe that these false accounts were willingly circulated by conspiratorial Christians in the early church does not bear up when one considers that many of their Jewish contemporaries were eyewitnesses to the 'alleged' events and the miracles proclaimed. Moreover, 11 of the apostles were martyred, and many early Christians were persecuted and killed by these unbelieving fellow Jews who thought it was blasphemy to claim Jesus as the Son of God. Would so many willingly sacrifice their lives for some lies in a text? Also, because the documents of the New Testament were written well within the lifetimes of skeptical witnesses, they would have attempted to set the record straight if early Christians had lied, and it is unlikely that a false Gospel would have spread so rapidly.

So, let's consider that Jesus was not God, but an ordinary man who accidentally or even intentionally fulfilled the prophecies. Arranging a colt to ride into the city might feasibly be arranged beforehand (Zechariah 9:9), after all, many of these prophecies were known about hundreds of years before. Once again, probability factors should be considered to get so many prophecies fulfilled in the exact manner as written, so let's look at the big picture. How feasible is it that an ordinary man can arrange the place of his birth; ensure that he came from the line of Judah; that his birth would trigger a massacre of infant boys in Israel; ensure that as a toddler his parents took him to Egypt; that he would live in Nazareth; or arrange for the Sanhedrin (the Jewish council of the religious leaders of the day who were against him) to pay exactly 30 pieces of silver to their accomplice; that the blood money would be used to buy a potter's field where his betrayer would commit suicide; or arrange his method of execution; be crucified alongside criminals; and to ensure that his legs remain unbroken; that they would pierce his side; to ensure that he would be given vinegar on a cross; that the soldiers would gamble for his garments; or that his disciples would scatter?

As you can see, many of these things a normal man could have no control of, and moreover, why would he want to, knowing the manner of his death to come?

Only God could foreknow these events, and someone who fulfilled all of them must be the Messiah, because it would be impossible to fulfill so many prophecies by chance. The arguments above only further demonstrate the divine inspiration and incredible unity of Scripture across its many books. The fact that God foreknew all of these, but still chose to become one of us and to die for us, displays His enormous love for us.

CAN THE BIBLE REALLY BE TRUSTED?
The great spiritual deliverance

The Bible is a pretty amazing book that contains incredible stories. It outlines the history of our world and the future history still to come. We should take its claims seriously. We should remember that the Bible's authors were much closer in time to the events they wrote about, and of course, for the majority, the events occurred in their own lifetimes. It is not reasonable to presume that these were fictitious stories, because their contemporaries would have soon squashed any untruths. But instead, the fact that these books were held in such high regard, preserved throughout generations, is a strong indicator of their authenticity. They were quickly copied so that the acts of God could be preserved for everyone else to read and be encouraged.

As we mentioned, the Old Testament made many predictions about the coming Messiah, Jesus Christ. Throughout history the Hebrew nation (Israel) repeatedly strayed from their covenant with God. When they were faithful to Him, He delivered them and prospered their land. When they were unfaithful and followed false religions, God punished them for their rebellion (sin).

Humans have a habit of making the same mistakes over and over, and so the Bible's history serves as a reminder that humankind is simply lost without our Creator. God in His mercy to us made a way for us to be reconciled back to Him. The Creator Himself (Colossians 1) sent a rescue mission and stepped out of His heavenly abode to pay the price for our offences to Him. The Bible records that when the Lord Jesus Christ willingly sacrificed Himself on a cruel Roman cross He paid for our sins. But that was not the end of it. He rose again from the dead—having power over death—thereby demonstrating that He is the author of life and the Genesis Creator that the very first book of the Bible revealed. And only the Genesis Creator can save us and restore our bodies from the dust. No other supposed holy book is like the Bible. Unlike all other religions, the Bible says that you don't have to earn your salvation—we can't anyway because in our sinful state we are incapable of pleasing God. No other guru or religious leader has risen from the dead—they are still in their graves. With all the overwhelming evidence that supports the Bible's history (including the death and resurrection of Christ), we should take its claims seriously. God's Word and the Christian faith it proclaims is unique in that it promises to us that:

> " … if you confess with your mouth that Jesus is Lord and believe in your heart that God raised him from the dead, you will be saved" (Romans 10:9).

You can do this today—right now. And how and why is it possible? Ephesians 2:8–9 explains:

> "For by grace you have been saved through faith. And this is not your own doing; it is the gift of God, not a result of works, so that no one may boast."

Grace has been described as God's unmerited favour upon humankind. We didn't deserve it, but His vast love for those He created ensured that we would not be lost from Him for eternity. However, you must have faith to believe this. Hebrews 11:6 states:

> "And without faith it is impossible to please him, for whoever would draw near to God must believe that he exists and that he rewards those who seek him."

Hopefully, this booklet has helped demonstrate to you the authenticity and validity of God's Word, the Bible, and that it can be trusted. We pray that this information is a start that can help you on your way to being reconciled to your Creator through faith in Jesus Christ. Do you recall at the beginning of this book we mentioned the three big questions? "Where did we come from?"; "Why are we here?"; and "Where are we going?" If you can start by believing God's Word from the very first verse, and that He is the Creator, it will help you find answers to the remaining two questions. There can be no greater call or purpose than to find out who your Creator is.

> "For God so loved the world, that he gave his only Son, that whoever believes in him should not perish but have eternal life. For God did not send his Son into the world to condemn the world, but in order that the world might be saved through him" (John 3:16–17).

References and Notes

1. Compare this to the evolutionary claims there was a big bang c. 14 billion years ago that no one was there to see.

2. See creation.com/genetics.

3. For more information go to CREATION.com which has many thousands of articles, many authored by real scientists, relating to these issues. Most are easily understood at a lay level and one can simply enquire by typing a question into the site's search engine.

4. Cosner, L., Our triune God, 18 October 2012, creation.com/triune-god.

5. For more information, see Cosner, L., Did Matthew misuse the Old Testament?, 24 December 2011, creation.com/matthew-ot-references.

6. Fructenbaum, A., *Messianic Christology*, Ariel Ministries, Tustin, California, USA, 1998, pp. 164–166.

7. Bates, G., *Alien Intrusion: UFOs and the Evolution Connection*, Creation Book Publishers, Atlanta, Georgia, December 2011, p. 106.

8. Mazar, L., Uncovering King David's Palace, *Moment Magazine,* April 2006. Accessed via archive.org, 2008-07-29.

9. 10 most read books in the world, squidoo.com/mostreadbooks, accessed 22 May 2013.

10. The worldwide status of Bible translation (2012); wycliffe.org/About/Statistics.aspx, as of 27 March 2013.

11. Osborne, G., *Revelation*, Baker Exegetical Commentary on the New Testament (Grand Rapids: Baker Academic, 2002), p. 799.

12. Slick, M., Manuscript evidence for superior New Testament reliability, carm.org/manuscript-evidence, as of 27 March 2013.

13. From Blomberg, C., 400,000 textual variants in the New Testament alone?, 30 September 2011; denverseminary.edu, 4 April 2013.

14. For more information, see Osborne, G., *Revelation*, Baker Exegetical Commentary on the New Testament, Baker Academic, Grand Rapids, Michigan, 2002, pp. 2–6.

15. Bible Translation, United Bible Society, unitedbiblesocieties.org, 6 November 2012.

16. *Science Speaks*, Stoner, P.W., and Newman, R.C., Moody Press, Online Edition revised November 2005, sciencespeaks.dstoner.net/index.html#c0, 3 April, 2013.

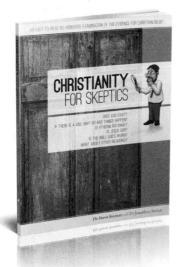

CREATION.com

For more information on creation/evolution and Bible-science issues

AUSTRALIA
Creation Ministries International (Australia)
PO Box 4545
Eight Mile Plains, Qld 4113

Phone: (07) 3340 9888
Fax: (07) 3340 9889
ABN 31 010 120 304

CANADA
Creation Ministries International (Canada)
300 Mill St,
Unit 7, Kitchener, ON N2M 5G8

Phone: (519) 746–7616
Orders & donations: 1-888-251-5360
Fax: (519) 746–7617

NEW ZEALAND
Creation Ministries International (NZ)
PO Box 39005
Howick, Auckland 2145

Phone/Fax: (09) 537 4818
A Registered Charitable Trust

SINGAPORE
Creation Ministries International (Singapore)
Clementi Central Post Office
PO Box 195
Singapore 911207

Phone: 9698 4292

SOUTH AFRICA
Creation Ministries International (SA)
PO Box 3349
Durbanville 7551

Phone: (021) 979 0107
Fax: (086) 519 0555

UK & Europe
*Creation Ministries International
(UK/Europe)*
15 Station St,
Whetstone, Leicestershire, LE8 6JS

Phone: 0845-6800-264

USA
Creation Ministries International (USA)
PO Box 350, Powder Springs,
GA 30127

Phone: 800-616-1264
Fax: (770) 439 9784

OTHER COUNTRIES
Creation Ministries International
PO Box 4545
Eight Mile Plains, Qld 4113
Australia

Phone: +617 3340 9888
Fax: +617 3340 9889